WordPress:

Beginner's Guide to Mastering WordPress
(With Easy Follow Step-by-Step Instructions)

Table of Contents

Introduction

Chapter 1: All About WordPress

Chapter 2: Hosting Your Site

Chapter 3: Building Your Site

Chapter 4: Securing Your Site

Chapter 5: Adding in Extras

Chapter 6: Blogging

Chapter 7: Maximizing Your SEO

Conclusion

Introduction

Congratulations on downloading *WordPress: Beginner's Guide to Mastering WordPress (With Easy Follow Step-by-Step Instructions)*, and thank you for doing so. When it comes to creating website for your small business, there is no better way of going about doing so than jumping into the WordPress ecosystem.

While not difficult by any measure, the process can seem quite arcane to those who have never undertaken it before which is why the following chapters will discuss everything you need to know about what makes WordPress the right choice to power your small business website. You will learn the ins and outs of choosing a host for your site, taking it from an idea to a reality, ensuring it is properly secured against those who might wish to do it harm and adding in extras including a dedicated blog, email newsletter signup section and store page. Finally, you will learn everything you need to know to maximize the effectiveness of your search engine optimization.

When you are done with the chapters in this book you will have a fully working website on your hands, but the journey won't end there. It is important to think of creating a website as a marathon, not a sprint, slow and steady wins the race.

There are plenty of books on this subject on the market, thanks again for choosing this one! Every effort was made to ensure it is full of as much useful information as possible, please enjoy!

Chapter 1: All About WordPress

As a small business owner, it is statistically likely that you can classify yourself in one of two ways. Either you know your brick and mortar store needs a website but you are dragging your feet on making it a reality or you have an extremely basic website that is never updated and at this point is doing little for you that a simple Google Maps search wouldn't provide except make you look bad in comparison to your competition. It doesn't matter on which side of the fence you fall; WordPress is  likely going to be the answer to your problems. While it was originally little more than a standard blogging platform, WordPress has since evolved into a full content management system that is sure to have the infrastructure to support the needs of your business, whatever those needs might be.

With so many options available to the average consumer with little more than a few flicks of the finger, not providing your business with an up to date online portal is thus directly hobbling the overall wealth producing capability of your business as a whole. Even if you feel as though your customer base is currently solid, studies show that, these days, 80 percent of customers choose a new business to patronize based on an online search and nothing more. This means that the longer you hold out on creating a fresh and relevant website, the greater the likelihood that your customer base is going to shrink will be. Consider how long you can survive an eroding customer base and a new WordPress site will suddenly start sounding a lot more promising.

Furthermore, a full 35 percent of all purchases are made online these days which means it doesn't matter what goods or services your business provides, if you are not offering them online as well as in an existing brick and mortar location then you are missing out on sales, no two ways about it. It doesn't matter how strong your sales numbers are currently, there are more potential customers out there just waiting for you to get your website up to snuff so they can start virtually examining your goods and services.

Having a modern, regularly updated website is akin to making a positive first impression when you meet someone for the first time. It shows that not only are you fully abreast of modern trends, but also that you are professional, you take pride in your company and you are always looking towards the future. On the other hand, if you have an obsolete site or no site at all you are essentially greeting potential customers in a stained and tattered bathrobe after you have just rolled out of bed. Put your best foot forward, put care into your website's image.

If you are hesitant about committing to something that sounds both time consuming and complicated, rest assured that WordPress has streamlined the website creation process so that anyone who knows what a modern website looks like should be able to duplicate the things they've seen with relative ease. If you still aren't convinced, consider the following reasons that have made WordPress one of the most popular website platforms in the world.

It can be set up in its entirety in less than 20 minutes: There is a reason that there are over 7 million websites based on the WordPress platform, the creation process is all based around drag and drop principles which means you don't need to worry about knowing how to code in HTML to create a professional looking site. The initial setup gives you access to plenty of customization options as well as plenty of add-ons to choose from automatically without having to track down each of the most popular options that many users go for manually.

Extremely easy to personalize: There are countless different ways that WordPress can be configured and themes that can be applied to the basic template to ensure that the website that you create for your business is going to be as unique as it is functional. Furthermore, there are options that will allow you to add on everything from a blog to an online store which means that you never need to step outside the basic implementation system even when you are looking for all of the bells and whistles.

Automatic SEO boost: Search engine optimization is the key to pulling in as many local customers who do a simple online search for nearby locations as possible. Luckily, each WordPress site is designed in such a way that it is as easy for search engines to find it as possible, giving it priority over sites built on other less efficient platforms.

Top notch security: WordPress takes user security extremely seriously which means that, aside from some initial additional measures, you will be able to sleep soundly knowing that your website will automatically download and implement new security patches as they are pushed out to the system.

Extensive community support: As previous mentioned, there are more than 7 million WordPress websites currently operating on the service which means that its community is as extensive as its web presence. This community is extremely active as well when it comes to creating free themes or supporting one another with tips and tricks, tools of the trade and extensive technical support.

One website for all of your needs: Modern WordPress sites automatically take into account the device that the user is accessing them through and update their look and interaction methods accordingly. When you create a WordPress site you don't need to worry about adjusting these details automatically, it is all taken care of for you.

It is an open source platform: WordPress is an open source platform which means that its source code is open to anyone to improve and iterate upon. When you sign up for a WordPress account you are only being limited by your own choices and you can do so secure in the knowledge that you never lose access to something you created due to outside influences. What's more, the platform has been around for over a decade something very few continuously update web platforms can claim. This is not a platform that is still experimenting with what it is offering or how it is going to reach new markets, this is a well-oiled machine that is ready to take your business into the modern age.

Plenty of options: It doesn't matter what you are looking to do, WordPress can take care of it for you. If you are looking to host multimedia content, you will be able to take care of it quickly and easily via the in page multimedia tools as well as in the dedicated Media Library function. Furthermore, it doesn't matter if you are looking to start creating email blasts or are looking to take a wider variety of online payments, WordPress has an easy way to make your plan a reality.

Low level of commitment: While you can host your site on WordPress for free, that option is not recommended, nor is their paid hosting service as it is somewhat overpriced. Luckily, you will be able to take your website to any hosting service that you like which means you are never going to be tied down to any service that you eventually feel you are no longer happy with.

It is free to try: Finally, it is important to keep in mind that you can go ahead and try it yourself before you commit to paying for anything. You can go ahead and create a basic site just to see what all of your specifics would look like on the page, and even let it go live, albeit with an unprofessional .wordpress.com URL. This should only ever be used as a way to test out your general ideas, your business is a professional operation and it needs a professional domain name to match. What's more, doing so will also give you access to even more customization options designed to allow you to more easily separate yourself from the pack.

Chapter 2: Hosting Your Site

Before you get started actually building your site, the first thing you are going to need to do is find a web hosting service that provides you with everything you need for a price that is reasonable for the market. Choosing the right web hosting service is a big responsibility and one that is not to be taken lightly which is why you should keep the following suggestions in mind to ensure the process proceeds as smoothly as possible.

Know what it is you are looking for: First and foremost, it is important to have a clear idea of what type of website you are looking to build as well as anything out of the ordinary that you might need. While most small businesses won't need to worry about anything besides whether or not the company you are looking into works with WordPress, you may want to look at caps and fees related to volume if you expect to be seeing a lot of traffic.

During this step of the process you are also going to want to think about not only what you are going to be using the website for right out of the gate but also what you plan on expanding into a year or more from now. If you are just looking for something that will get you started, then what is known as a shared hosting account will work just fine. Shared hosting just means you get less dedicated service for your site but with the amount of traffic you are likely going to be receiving this should not be an issue. You should easily be able to find this type of hosting for a starter price of less than $5 per month.

Do your homework: Once you know what is that you are going to need from the web host that you choose, the next thing you will need to do is look into any recommended web hosting services that your friends or family use on a regular basis. Getting a reliable recommendation can save you a lot of time and effort while also allowing you to move forward with confidence knowing with certainty that you made the right choice. If you aren't able to proceed with a recommendation, you are going to instead want to start narrowing down potential options by reading lots of online customer reviews. While you will not want to necessarily disqualify a given company just because of a few bad reviews, you will want to keep an eye out for emerging trends that all point to the fact that you would be better off moving in a different direction.

With the field narrowed significantly, it will then be worth your time to looking into the specific details of the remaining choices. First and foremost, you are going to want to ensure that the web host is going to be operating constantly will a network connection that is proven stable at least 99.5 percent of the time. Tools for doing this can be found online for free with a simple web search. Other than that, you will want to ensure that any account you sign up for allows you access to multiple domain names as well, generally with at least one for free. Typically, you can expect to be able to use anywhere from 10 to 25 domains with a single shared use account. Finally, you will want to ensure that you have access to enough storage for what you will be using this site for, if you plan on using lots of high resolution photos or video you may need to consider purchasing more than the minimum available amount of space.

Look into long term pricing: While it is perfectly normal for an initial year of hosting fees to go for $40 or less, it is important to take the time to look into what the cost is going to be a year or so down the road as these fees typically increase significantly after the honeymoon period is over. You should still be able to find monthly costs under $10, but only if you do your homework before you are already committed.

Finding the perfect domain name
As previously mentioned, you will likely get at least one free domain name with your hosting plan, so it is important to put the proper amount of thought into so that it is as impactful and useful of a free marketing tool as possible. When it comes to choosing the right name, the obvious choice is the name of your company, but only if that name is relatively short and also easy to spell and pronounce. If your company name doesn't meet these criteria, or if the name that is your first choice is already taken, then you may want to consider the guidelines for choosing a great domain name.

Make sure it is easily understood when spoken aloud: You want it to be as easy for people to link your domain name with your website and your business as possible which means you are going to want to avoid using confusing number to letter replacements or single letter abbreviations no matter what. If you think you have found the perfect domain name only to have it snatched out from under you, start over and avoid the temptation to abbreviate as the odds are good you will ultimately waste advertising sending potential customers to the competition. This also means that you will want to leave out numbers of any type as it will be impossible to tell if the speaker is referring to the number in question or the written word version of the number.

Shorter is better: While you want a short URL, you also want something memorable so at least a full word is best. You will want to stick to a domain that is three words or less, anything more and you run the risk of potential customers mishearing or mistyping the URL and ruining all of your hard work with their ignorance.

Use keywords and phrases: While this won't be possible in all situations, you should start off by trying to procure a URL related to keywords or phrases that people use when trying to find details on the type of business you are in. If the basic keywords are taken, you might still be able to get a local variation including the keyword plus your city, your state, or both.

Be clever but not too clever: While you will certainly want to make the extra effort to ensure that your domain name is going to be catchy enough to outdo the competition, it is important that you don't become so focused on being clever that you put too much priority on it and lose sight of the benefits of having a short and simple name as well. It is important to be clever, but you will never want form to supersede function. Additionally, you are going to want to share your clever name with some friends and family members to ensure you are not too close to the matter at hand and that it tracks with a wider audience.

Do a bit of research: Once you come up with a few different names that you like that are not currently being used by anyone else, the last thing you are going to want to do is plug each of the terms you came up with into your search engine of choice, just to see what type of results you come up with. If any of your terms come back as relating to a major company, or even just an established brand, it is better to back off and come up with something else at this early stage of the game rather than potentially deal with an extended legal battle further down the line.

Chapter 3: Building Your Site

WordPress has made a name for itself over the years for its easy to manage installation process that in many cases will take a grand total of five minutes or less to complete successfully. However, it does require a somewhat above average degree of computer literacy which means that for the easiest time of it possible, it is best to choose a hosting company that uses a WordPress auto installer instead. If you choose to go it alone and install WordPress by yourself, detailed instructions for doing so can be found at WordPress.org. The most commonly used autoinstallers are Softaculous, Insallatron, Fantastico and APS and auto installer instructions for each can be found below.

APS: If you are using a Plesk control panel then the first thing you are going to want to do is to log into your account before selecting the tab labeled Applications. This will cause a new screen to open and from there you will want to choose the option to install WordPress. You will have the option for a simple or a detailed installation process if you are interested in setting specific parameters outside of the default. All you need to do is choose the option for a Quick Install and WordPress will be installed.

Fantastico: To install WordPress via Fantastico, the first thing you are going to want to do is to log into the account you set up with cPanel before choosing the Fantastico option. You will then be able to find the option for WordPress underneath the category labeled Blogs. From there, all that is left is to select the option for a new installation, fill in the details of your choice and select submit for your will to be made manifest in the form of a fresh WordPress site.

Installatron: Installatron is a great choice for those who are setting up a WordPress site for the very first time because it can be used with numerous different web hosting providers but is also available for anyone to use at Insallatron.com. If you are installing it through a control panel, then you will simply want to locate Installatron on the control panel and select the install WordPress option. You will then be prompted to confirm the installation and away you go.

If, on the other hand, you plan on using Installatron directly from its website then you will want to start by finding the WordPress option on the site and then selecting the option to Install This Application. You will then need to enter your hosting account details as well as your database information. You will then simply need to confirm the installation and you will be up and running in no time.

Softaculous: To install WordPress using this program you will simply log into your web hosting account before seeking out the Services/Software tab to find Softaculous. After that, you will want to select the category for Blogs where WordPress will be located. Click the option to install, fill in the required information, submit it and you are ready to go.

Choosing a theme
Logging into the backend of your site after you have installed WordPress appropriately will now give you access to a wide variety of personalization options for your new site, though perhaps none are more important than choosing the right theme to accurately reflect your site. The theme you choose will change the way your site functions, in some cases, along with most definitely changing the way it looks and it is important to try out several different ones before settling on the one that is right for you. There are both free and paid theme options available, though you should be able to find something to get you started without having to directly put any money down right off of the bat.

Looking for a new theme: In order to find a theme for your new site, all you need to do is login to your new WordPress backend and find the option for Appearance on the left hand side of the screen. From there you will see that Themes is the first option that is provided to you. Clicking this option will present you with a plethora of options, so to slim them down somewhat you are going to want to select the Add New option at the top of the screen.

This, in turn, will bring up a detailed search function with plenty of different options including broad categories like newest themes, most popular themes, featured themes and more. You will also have options to choose the primary colors that you are interested in, various different types of layout emphasis, important features to be highlighted and even festive seasonal and holiday based options.

When it comes to choosing the perfect theme for you, the first thing that you are going to want to consider is choosing something that is clean and simple without a lot of flash and clutter. It is important to consider the look of modern websites when creating your own as you are going to want something that attracts customers by showing them that you are familiar with current trends and up to date on whatever it is you plan on selling as opposed to things that are old hat.

You are going to want to focus on themes that have only a few primary colors and then a few secondary colors that complement the first. Ideally these colors are going to be on brand with your business in general, it is important to keep things uniform to really drive the message behind your brand home for the best results.

Installing a free theme: Once you come across a theme that you think has potential, all you need to do is mouse over the related picture and then either choose the preview button to see what you page would look like with the given template or the install button if you are ready to go ahead and pull the trigger directly. Once you click the install button you will see a message from WordPress indicating the success of the process as well as an option to either preview the theme or to Activate it.

You must choose the Activate button to get the theme up and running on your page. When you choose some themes that have a host of promised additional features you will find that the installation activates the basic features of the theme while the more advanced options will often have their own secondary menu to configure for the full scope of the results. These secondary menus are typically added either under the appearance submenu or as their own option on the admin panel on the left side of the screen.

Installing a paid theme: If you instead plan on using a third party company to either create or supply you with a custom template, then the process for doing so is still quite simple, just a little different from the steps outlined above. First, you are going to want to download the theme that you paid for to your hard drive. You will then want to log into your WordPress account and select the option for Themes found under the Appearance section of the admin panel on the left side of the screen.

You will still want to choose the Add Themes button at the top of the screen only this type you will want to seek out the Upload theme button instead. You will then want to select the file that you have chosen before selecting the option to Install Now. After the theme has finished installing you will then have the option to either Activate it or see a Live Preview on Your site. You will need to choose the activate option in order to complete the installation process.

Chapter 4: Securing Your Site

While the WordPress platform automatically goes to decent lengths to ensure the security of every one of the sites that are powered by its network, the fact of the matter is that with so many different sites operating under its banner, the platform as a whole is going to be a natural target for hackers from all sides. Luckily, there is more that you can do outside of the standard security procedures to give yourself an edge against those who might potentially want to cause you and your website harm. Give the following suggestions a try and hackers will find your site to be much more difficult to tamper with than it might naturally be.

Secure the login

It is very easy to find the login page to the backend of any WordPress sites because they are all essentially the same by default. As such, if you are worried about adding extra security to your site the first thing you should do is to add an extra layer of security your login page. Regardless of what other types of precautions you ultimately choose to take with your site, it is important to always make a point of changing your passwords regularly to ensure that hackers have as little existing information to go on as possible when it comes to breaking into your site.

Limit login attempts: The easiest way to stop a brute force attack on your website's backend is to simply limit the number of login attempt chances you have to match the correct username with the correct password at login before a timed lockout occurs. This way, a hacker won't be able to run a program that just tries countless passwords until something clicks and instead you will be notified of the failed attempts. An easy way to enact this feature is by downloading the plugin named iThemes Security. This plugin will allow you to ban failed attempts based on IP address while also offering up other functions as well.

Add additional authentication: If you are looking for a more complex solution, you can also add a second required layer of authentication to your login page. This way you can ensure that anyone who logs into your backend has not just your username and password, but also the answer to a secret question, code or set of characters that you specify. You can set up a secondary authentication system using the WP Google Authenticator found in the free plugin section of the WordPress achieve.

Change the URL you use to login: As previously noted, it is very easy to guess the standard backend login URL for most WordPress websites as it is set to a standard format by default. As such, if you change your login URL you automatically make it more difficult for those with malicious intent to begin to penetrate your defenses. Changing this login URL to something unique instead of the standard option can also be accomplished via the iThemes Security plugin that was mentioned above.

Add security to the dashboard

As the admin dashboard is naturally the most secure part of any WordPress page, it is the part that hackers are prone to trying to attack the most as provides the greatest sense of accomplishment when successfully cracked. What's worse, if they make it into this section of your website they will have the ability to do a massive amount of damage in a very short period of time. This is why it is so important to ensure your admin panel security is up to snuff with these extra precautions.

Add wp-admin directory security: The directory labeled wp-admin is the beating heart of your website which means irreparable damage can be done if it is pierced with ill intent. You can start making it more difficult to access by adding a layer of password protection limiting access rights to it. To add a password to this part of your site you can download the plugin named AskApache Password Protect. This plugin goes ahead and creates a separate password file as well as encrypting the password and offering you configurable file permission options.

Encrypt data with SSL: Adding a secure socket layer (SSL) certificate to your admin panel will help to further secure the data that users submit to your server which will make it more difficult for hackers to get a foothold into your system. Your hosting company likely offers SSL certificates for an extra fee, or sometimes for free, or there are numerous different high quality open source options available online as well. As an added bonus, implementing this security step will improve your Google ranking as sites with an SSL certificate are given preferential status when search results are returned.

Force users to be careful: If you allow users to create accounts on your site, then this means you are going to be giving them limited access to your backend for various purposes. When you make the decision to implement this feature it is important that you take the time to enforce a rule requiring strong passwords so that you aren't allowing weak links in your chain to form. A good way to do this is to download the plugin named Force Strong Passwords which, as the name implies, forces users to pick secure passwords when creating an account.

Always choose a new username: When you create your WordPress account you will be asked to create a password but your username can remain simply Admin if you let it. This is always going to be a poor choice, however, as anything that remains set to the default setting is going to make it easier for hackers to break into your account. Don't do the hackers any favors, always change your username to anything besides the default option and do so as quickly as possible.

Add data base security

All of the information that populates your website, including usernames and any collected details are stored in your database; this data is valuable and deserves to be treated as such. Ensure it is well protected by implementing the following additional security measures.

Rename the database prefix: The database prefix is another automatically standardized naming convention that renaming will go a long way to increasing your baseline security. Leaving this prefix set to the default option will make it possible to attack your database via an SQL injection attack. Luckily, this can easily be prevented by changing this prefix (wp- by default) to literally anything else that you will be sure to remember. If you have already chosen the default setting, then you can easily change it by using iThemes Security once again.

Frequently backup your site: Regardless of how secure you feel your site is in the moment, there is always room for something, somewhere, to go wrong. As such, it is important that you keep an offline backup of your website somewhere safe so that you can scrap the current version and retry with a fresh variation instead. While there are plenty of well-reviewed free options in this regard, one of the most commonly used paid version is called VaultPress and it will back up your entire site every 30 minutes while checking your entire site for malware in the interim.

Set a third password: When it comes to setting a password for your database it is important to pick something outside of the password that use to access any other part of your site. While you might be running out of passwords at this point, a random password generator is always going to be a quick and easy way to come up with new ideas.

Chapter 5: Adding in Extras

Integrating an email list

If you are interested in regularly communicating with your customers and users via email, then the most common way that you can hope to do so is with the use of the MailChimp communication platform. MailChimp can be activated from the admin dashboard and can provide you with a wide variety of tools to ensure you can 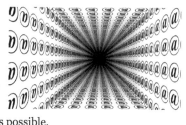 communicate with your user base as easily as possible.

MailChimp and WordPress integration comes in two main categories, the first and easiest to use is the email subscription form. The easiest way to gain access to a simple subscription form that your users can sign up for directly from your site is through the use of the MailChimp for WordPress plugin. The results of this plugin are a variety of extremely easy to customize forms that can be formatted to fit your current theme in almost all situations.

With the MailChimp plugin downloaded, the next thing you will want to do is head on over to MailChimp.com and sign up for an account. From the MailChimp dashboard you are then going to want to do two different things, first you will want to create a list for the WordPress plugin to automatically populate, and second you will want to find your MailChimp API as the WordPress plugin will need it in order to work properly. To find your MailChimp API you will want to start by logging into your MailChimp account before selecting the Account Name option on the left side of the screen. You will then want to select the option for extras where you can then select the API keys option.

With this process out of the way your MailChimp plugin and your MailChimp account should now be communicating properly allowing users to your site to sign up for your email newsletter automatically. Back in the plugin settings, after entering in the API details you will then want to ensure the box for the correct email newsletter is provided, and that the option to have subscribers confirm their email address is checked. You will also have the option to determine if you are interested in adding a variety of other forms to the plugin as well depending on your personal preferences. You will also be able to create a label for the subscription plugin on your site as well as determining the actual style and font the plugin will use.

The final list of options is going to look confusing because it allows users to manually input HTML code but that isn't the only way you can interact with the screen so it is much less of a hassle than it looks. All you need to concern yourself with is adding a new field related to first name, last name and email address and the plugin should take care of the rest.

It is important to keep in mind that there is both a free and a paid version of this application but as a small business owner who is just getting their feet wet online the free version should provide you with more than enough options to adequately meet your needs. Furthermore, it is important to keep in mind that the MailChimp for Wordpress plugin is not the official MailChimp WordPress plugin as that plugin has a very low overall user rating. While this can be confusing, as long as you search the list of plugins for MailChimp, and then proceed with the plugin that has a very high and not a very low user rating you should be fine. The preferred plugin currently has a 4.9 user rating while the lesser used plugin is sitting around a 2 so there is very little room for confusion as long as you go into the process with the understanding of what you are looking for.

Creating an online store space
WooCommerce is the current leading name in the WordPress digital store plugin space. WooCommerce is built from the ground up for use with sites that are built using WordPress which means it naturally integrates into many themes more easily than other digital commerce platforms that have been retrofitted to work with the service. WooCommerce works with for any type of product from physical, to digital and every page of your store will transition seamlessly regardless if users are accessing your content via a mobile or traditional platform. Furthermore, there are numerous different extensions that you can further bolt onto the system to ensure an even greater range of personalization options.

Installing WooCommerce: If you are interested in selling products on your WordPress page through WooCommerce, the first thing you are going to want to do is search for WooCommerce in the plugins store. You will then want to download the plugin and install it before activating it as well. You will then need to install a secondary plugin called WooCommerce pages so that you can add products to your WooCommerce store.

Adding products: Once all this has been installed you will see that your admin dashboard now has two new tabs that have been added to the side menu, on for products and one titled WooCommerce. WooCommerce is where you will find your general setting and Products is where you will find settings specific to the products you are selling. To get started you are going to awn to choose the products tab and then the option to add products.

The resulting screen will show you what the current listing looks like including the name of the product, any pictures, a description and any reviews that have been left regarding it. You will want to fill in all of these fields as thoroughly as you can to ensure that as many people click through to the product as possible. The higher the click through rate, the higher the overall sales rate is going to be.

Product Data: If you scroll lower on the page underneath the post editor you will find a widget that is labeled Product Data. This widget will let you determine several important facts about the product, including whether or not it is actually something real that exists in the world or if it is only a digital product. You will also have the option to enter the price, the price when the item is on sale and any SKU number the product might have. You will also have the option of filling in shipping information as well as the overall number of each item that is available and if backorders can be taken.

Under the tab marked Linked Products you will also find the ability to connect products via things like product groupings, cross selling or upselling. There is also a tab labeled Attributes that allows you to list traits of the product in question that will be visible via the additional information tab on each product page.

Short Product Description: Underneath the space for Product Data you will find an option to include a short description of the product that will be visible underneath the picture and the product title. This is also where you will find options to add relevant tags and metadata to the product as well as add in any and all relevant pictures. Finally, you will be given a preview of the end result and asked to confirm your choices.

WooCommerce Tab: Underneath the WooCommerce tab you will find things like a list of current pending orders, which will appear under the Orders option. You will be able to organize shipping details from this screen as well as determine the specifics of any coupons you are currently running. Finally, the Reports option will provide you with detailed information regarding different products as well as registered customers.

Chapter 6: Blogging

Regardless of what type of business you are
running, you can be doing more to take advantage
of the free advertising that naturally comes along
with running a blog on your website as well.
While the information that is presented on your
homepage will naturally take the form of a blog by
default, you can also create something that is
more structured for your blogging activities by
following the steps outlined below.

Create a page for your blog

Create a pair of new pages: As previously mentioned, the default home page on
a new WordPress website is automatically set up to be a blog page. If you instead
prefer to have a separate place for your blog entries, the first thing you are going
to want to do is setup two new pages by using the admin dashboard, specifically
the Pages option to create new pages. The first of these pages should be titled
Home. After adding in a title you will want to find the Page Attributes box on the
right side of the screen and then choose the Front Page Template from the
template options on the resulting page.

You will then want to title the second page that you created Blog. Depending on
the template that you have decided to go with, you may be able to find an option
under templates that is blog specific, otherwise the standard template is perfectly
acceptable. You will want to ensure that the options for trackbacks as well as
comments are deselected in this instance.

Have WordPress use the pages you created properly: After you have created and
populated a new homepage for your WordPress site to link to and a blog page to
be filled in over time, you will then want to ensure that they are displayed
properly. To do that you will want to choose the Settings option from the Admin
dashboard before selecting the suite of options labeled Reading. Under the option
for Front Page you will want to select your new homepage and under Post pages
you will want to include your page labeled Blog. You will then want to be sure to
save your changes.

Show your blog on the navigation menu: All that is left to do is to go back to the
admin dashboard before selecting the option for Appearance before selecting the
option labeled Menus. This is the option that allows you to determine which
pages show up in the navigation menu.

Creating viable blog content

Regardless of what your small business is selling, you can easily benefit from adding a blog to your site and updating it regularly. First, it will make it easier to get customers interested in trying out your email newsletters assuming you regularly create the type of content that people are interested in reading. Second, when done properly it can easily create target advertising for specific products and finally, it can be used to make you appear as though you are the leading expert in a given topic which will naturally lead to an increase in brand awareness and eventually sales.

Becoming an expert: If it currently seems farfetched to consider yourself an expert in any products or services that you are currently providing, then your customers are currently thinking the same thing. The first step to getting this surefire marketing solution to start working for you is to choose a niche related to the products and services that you currently offer in your store. When it comes to choosing a niche you are going to want something that is broad enough to get a reasonable amount of true support while at the same time being under the radar enough that the space is not yet clogged with blogs on the topic. With a topic in mind, the next thing you are going to want to do is to research everything you can about it until you have a decent grasp on all of the basics as well as some intermediate concepts as well.

Start blogging: Once you have reached a general baseline of knowledge, the next thing you are going to need to do is to start blogging every single day about the niche that you have landed on. You can start with the basic knowledge that you have recently learned, but once you have exhausted that you will then want to start learning more and more about the topic with each blog post. While this will certainly be time consuming, given enough regular posts your site will start popping up in the upper echelons of the search engine results for the topic in question and as an added bonus you will gain a greater knowledge in a related field as well as a new potential revenue stream in niche products.

Keep blogging: It is important to keep up the blog on a regular basis (taking weekends off is fine) and really commit to it in the long term if you plan on starting it up at all. A regularly updated blog shows that you are serious about your website and about the topic that you are writing about. At the same time, a blog that is updated several times to start and then never again, or only sporadically, will make viewers assume that you don't update your website regularly or care about it that much at all. As such, if you do not think that you can commit to a steady output of blog content then you are likely going to be better off not starting a business blog in the first place.

Keep direct advertising content to a minimum: While every now and then if you get a particularly interesting new product in then by all means you can blog about it as long as you can come up with a reason for doing so besides the fact that it is a new item in your store. Especially early on, it is important to keep this type of content to a minimum, however, as it can be easy to turn new readers off if they feel as though all you are doing is plugging items that are in your store. A good rule is that one blog post in ten can contain content that is not purely informational, though your readers should never feel as though all they are reading is a hard sell.

Spread the word: After you have amassed a fair amount of content, you are going to want to start a viral marketing campaign for yourself by seeking out forums and other online hangouts of the target audience for your niche and becoming a regular fixture in them. This is especially useful in forums as you can answer questions that people have and then include a link to your site where the user can learn more. While this won't cause major new streams of traffic to start pouring in immediately, over time if enough people see your name connected to a given niche they will start to connect the dots and bring their discretionary spending dollars along with them.

Additionally, you will want to reach out to other bloggers in the niche space and offer to write guest blogs for them as well. While creating content for your competition might initially seem like the last thing you are going to want to do, the reality is that the amount of credibility that you gain by being seen on other relevant sites more than makes up for the favor you are doing for the other blogger. Nothing says that you are an expert in a field like guesting on another popular blog and all of the extra hits you will get when these types of things post will prove this point time and again.

Chapter 7: Maximizing Your SEO

Once your site is successfully up and running it is important that you do everything in your power to ensure that your search engine optimization (SEO) is on point in order to ensure that you get as many new potential customers to your landing page as possible. Bing and Google both work through a process that involves sending automated web crawling programs out into the wilds of the internet to take note of the relevant  information that is stored on each page. That information, in turn, is used to create the search results that you see when you plug a search term into your favorite search engine.

With that in mind, SEO can then be thought of as the ways that you optimize your website for use by those automated programs so that it is easier for them to see the full breadth of your site, ensuring that it is then ranked higher in related searches. This is where keywords come in, though now they are often thought of as key phrases instead and it is why it is important for you to include them with every blog post, for the site itself and on every product page in your online store. Adding keywords for the site itself can be done from the Metatags option and each new post will have the option to add in keywords or phrases for the post as well.

Choosing the best keywords for the job
When you are looking for the keywords that will ultimately concisely and effectively define what your website is all about, it is important that you take the time to consider how you see your online business and what sets it apart from its competition. It is important to not take this decision lightly and instead start by keeping the following tips in mind to ensure the best results.

Find the right amount of specificity: When it comes to choosing keywords it is important to not choose words that are so broad that they are meaningless when it comes to narrowing down a search field, while also ensuring that the words and phrases that you land on are common enough that there is a chance your potential customers will actually use them when it comes time for them to use the search function on your site.

As an example, if you were to run a business that sells healthy cat food then you would want to stay away from terms like food or cat and instead use specific adjectives that describe the food as a jumping off point. As a general rule, you are likely going to find the most success with key phrases that are anywhere from two to four words in length. Unless the words are enough to truly help your page stand out, single keywords will not prove overly effective in this day and age.

Before you settle on the key phrases for your entire site, it is important that you do the right type of research beforehand to ensure that the words you are using have enough hits that it proves they are actually being used while at the same time not flooding you with so many major businesses on the first page of the search results, or even worse one or two major retailers for the entire first page, then you will want to think about moving in another direction instead. It is important to not take specific keywords and phrases too personally and instead move on to more fruitful ground rather than trying to directly duke it out with another company that is already established in the market.

Don't be afraid to repeat key phrases: While not every key phrase that you come up with is going to generate the types of search engine traffic that you are looking for, if you come upon something that seems particularly effective, there is nothing wrong with connecting it to several different pages, as long as they all have something that is clearly in common with one another. You will want to ensure that the key phrase in question is only used in relevant circumstances if you want it to maintain its efficacy.

Always create keywords and phrases to support your overall SEO strategy: It is important that every new piece of content that you create for your site, the more the better as that is also a factor in search result placement, is done with an eye towards what your SEO strategy currently is and what tags and phrases that you use on the regular can accurately be used in the situation in question. Improving your SEO ranking requires lots of planning, forethought and follow through and that should include every single new piece of content that you add to your site, every time.

Maximize your website's SEO
With the right types of keywords in place, there are still several other things you can do in order to ensure your website is as tuned to SEO as possible.

Make sure your site loads quickly: While you are going to want to ensure that every product that you are selling has at least one quality picture, that doesn't mean that picture is going to need to be extremely large as too many large pictures can make it difficult for your pages to load at a reasonable rate, hurting your page ranking results in the process. It is important to check this type of usability not just in the traditional form of the website, but in the mobile version as well. Keep in mind that society today is all about instant gratification, if you take too long to show people what it is you have to offer, you are essentially throwing away a potential sale.

Keep usage in mind: More and more, search engines are prioritizing websites that users spend a longer period of time on which means that ease of use and quality of content is going to a long way towards getting your site where it needs to be. This means that not only are you going to want to ensure that you create enough blog content to keep people on your site for a prolonged period of time, you also want to make sure that they can easily find anything else they are looking for. To that end, it is important to only choose a theme that presents all of the relevant information as clearly as possible as anything that is too busy is only going to get in the way of legibility.

Additionally, you will want to ensure that every time that you create a link to another page on your site or to another page online that the link you created actually goes where you expect it too. Furthermore, you are going to want to ensure that when you are blogging you make it a point of regularly linking to several of your other blogs in the text of the current blog as this type of interlinking structure is something that web crawlers love to see.

Keep the little things in mind: While it can be easy to give proper key phrases to all of your blog posts, you are also going to want to think about the little things as well such as choosing the option to have unique URLs for every page as well as making a point of always including descriptions and key phrases for all of your pictures as well as the pages that they are connected to. While individually they might not be worth much extra result rankings, but when added to the whole they can easily push you over the top.

Conclusion

Thank for making it through to the end of *WordPress: Beginner's Guide to Mastering WordPress (With Easy Follow Step-by-Step Instructions)*, let's hope it was informative and able to provide you with all of the tools you need to achieve your goals whatever it is that they may be. Just because you've finished this book doesn't mean there is nothing left to learn on the topic, expanding your horizons is the only way to find the mastery you seek.

The next step is to stop reading already and to get ready to create a WordPress site that is truly unique to you and your business. Instead of getting started directly, however, you might find that you will benefit from doing a bit of planning when it comes to what the overall look and feel of the site in question are going to be like. The more time that you put into determining the details you want to include in your site early on, the easier it will be to make it all into a reality when the moment of truth finally arrives.

Remember, modern website design is all about a less is more mentality which means that you are going to want to go with a few major design choices offset by several subtle variations on the same theme. Don't forget, there are plenty of themes to choose from and even if you don't choose a particular theme there is generally something you can learn from it no matter what. The broader your range of influences, the more eye catching your site is sure to ultimately be.

Finally, if you found this book useful in anyway, a review on Amazon is always appreciated!

Description

When it comes to creating a modern looking website that is packed with as much functionality as possible, there is no better choice for a content management system than WordPress. There are currently more than 7 million sites online that are powered by WordPress and if you are interested in seeing what all of the fuss is about, then *WordPress: Beginner's Guide to Mastering WordPress (With Easy Follow Step-by-Step Instructions)* is the book that you have been waiting for.

First created as a blogging service in 2003, WordPress has since gone on to be one of the primary platforms of the last decade and now offers everything from online stores, to traditional websites, to the blogging services that originally put it on the map. Inside you will find everything you need to get started with your very own WordPress site for absolutely no upfront costs. When you are ready to put your money where your mouth is you will also learn about the various options you have when it comes to hosting your site as well as building your site to ensure it is as effective as possible. You will also learn how to create a blog that people are actually going to want to read while all the while maximizing your SEO in the process.

Studies show that these days' businesses that do not have a modern and up to date website are at a huge disadvantage compared to their competitors. So, what are you waiting for? Don't be left in the dust, join the digital revolution and buy this book today!

Inside you will find
- Secrets to securing your site so thoroughly that no hacker will be able to get through
- The most effective way to utilize a blog to grow your business. Period.
- The best ways to find the best web host for your site
- *And more...*

www.ingramcontent.com/pod-product-compliance
Lightning Source LLC
Chambersburg PA
CBHW060938050326
40689CB00013B/3143